COOL Chemistry Concoctions

COOL

Chemistry Concoctions

50 Formulas that Fizz, Foam, Splatter & Ooze

Joe Rhatigan
&
Veronika Alice Gunter

Illustrated by
Tom LaBaff

LARK BOOKS
A Division of Sterling Publishing Co., Inc.
New York

Creative Director
CELIA NARANJO

Cover Designer
BARBARA ZARETSKY

Illustrator
TOM LABAFF

Book Design &
Production
CELIA NARANJO

Production Assistance
SHANNON YOKELEY
BILJANA BOSEVSKA

Editorial Assistance
DELORES GOSNELL
RAIN NEWCOMB

Chemistry Consultant
JENNIFER THOMAS

Rhatigan, Joe.
    Cool chemistry concoctions : 50 formulas that fizz, foam, splatter & ooze
/ Joe Rhatigan & Veronika Alice Gunter ; illustrated by Tom LaBaff.— 1st ed.
        p. cm.
    Includes index.
    ISBN 1-57990-620-6 (hardback)
    1. Science—Experiments—Juvenile literature. I. Gunter, Veronika Alice.
II. LaBaff, Tom, ill. III. Title.
Q164.R476 2005
540'.78—dc22

                                                        2004013287

10 9 8 7 6 5 4 3 2 1

First Edition

Published by Lark Books, a division of
Sterling Publishing Co., Inc.
387 Park Avenue South, New York, N.Y. 10016

© 2005, Lark Books
Illustrations © Tom LaBaff

Distributed in Canada by Sterling Publishing,
c/o Canadian Manda Group, 165 Dufferin Street,
Toronto, Ontario, Canada M6K 3H6

Distributed in the U.K. by Guild of Master Craftsman Publications Ltd.,
Castle Place, 166 High Street, Lewes, East Sussex, England, BN7 1XU
Tel: (+ 44) 1273 477374, Fax: (+ 44) 1273 478606, Email: pubs@thegmcgroup.com,
Web: www.gmcpublications.com

Distributed in Australia by Capricorn Link (Australia) Pty Ltd.,
P.O. Box 704, Windsor, NSW 2756 Australia

If you have questions or comments about this book, please contact:
Lark Books
67 Broadway
Asheville, NC 28801
(828) 253-0467

Manufactured in China

ISBN: 1-57990-620-6

Contents

INTRODUCTION 6
ALL ABOUT CHEMISTRY 8
LAB RULES 10

THE CONCOCTIONS
Rock-My-World Candy 12
Cave Chemistry 14
Fossil-Making Fun 16
Volcano 17
What Makes Your Pop Pop? 18
Soda Slobber 19
Do-It Itself Balloon 20
Homemade Bubble Stuff 21
Bubble Business 22
In the Bag 24
Exploding Water Bomb 25
Head Shrinker 26
Pass the Salt, Mummy! 27
Crystal Garden 28
Giant Gems 29
Bendable Bones 30
Bouncing Egg 31
Eggshell Eaters 32
Lab Sleuths 33
Decode This! 34
Fistful of Slime 36
Slime It Is 37
'Snot for Everyone 38
Clean Green Slime 39
Bob the Bouncing Blob 40
Powder-Powered Projectile 42

Gas Power! 43
Disappearing Acts 44
Color-Change Tricks 46
Color Chromatography 48
Super Suds 50
Sudsational Chemistry 51
Crush Me If You Can 52
Lava Lamps 54
Suspended Animation 56
Moo-vable Milk 57
Geyser 58
Real Geysers 59
Paint Party 60
Fountain Fun 62
Full of Hot Air 63
Indication Chemistry 64
Doubling Dough Balls 66
Cupcake Chemistry 67
Float This 68
Rust In Peace 70
Penny Plastic Surgery 71
Going Where No Egg Has Gone Before 72
Fire Extinguisher 73
Air Freshener Bubbles 74

SMELL YA LATER 75
GLOSSARY 76
METRIC CONVERSIONS 78
ACKNOWLEDGMENTS 79
INDEX 80

The REAL Reason Scientists Wear Lab Coats
(or, Why This Book is AWESOME)

I, **Lucinda Bright,** after performing multiple experiments and researching in the best libraries in my hometown (okay, the only library in my hometown), have irrefutable evidence that explains once and for all why scientists wear lab coats. Yes, yes, you probably think scientists wear lab coats because science can be a bit messy sometimes. Obvious hypothesis, but greater minds (like mine) know better. My studies have led me to the conclusion that lab coats look way cool. In fact, everyone should have one—even people who aren't scientists. Now, what does this have to do with this book? I guess that's an okay question, but the answer is: not much.

Well, speaking of this book, my team of scientific experts (my assistants ... I mean friends ... **Jessie** and **Tidy Tim**) and I have put together 50 of the coolest chemistry con-coctions known to humankind—they fizz, they bubble, they explode, they splatter. And we did it just for you.

These concoctions will amaze, astound, and even confuse you. That's what good science can do. And for your eager, curious mind, we have figured out why these concoctions are doing what they're doing—the science behind the fun!

You can concoct most of these wonders on your own. Simply gather the stuff needed and follow the instructions. Then, whether you're elbow deep in a Fistful of Slime (page 36) or seeking cover from your Geyser (page 58), you'll be amazed. I promise.

Every now and then **my dad, Dr. Ignatius B. Bright,** is going to ask you to get an adult to give you a hand. Don't skip that part—experiments can be tricky, and complicated, and it's always best to practice caution.

So, get ready for some good, messy science. Lab coat optional. If I had more room here, I'd love to tell you all about lab goggles…

All About Chemistry

When you hear the word "chemical" what do you think of? Is it the 12-syllable ingredients found in junk food? How about green radioactive slime oozing out of giant barrels? A mad scientist with a bubbling concoction that will turn him into some sort of wolf dude? Yes, this is all chemistry (except for the wolf dude concoction). But chemistry is so much more. In fact, chemistry is the study of all substances—all the stuff in the universe, which chemists like to call *matter*. If it takes up space and has weight, it's usually matter, and chemistry has something to do with it.

Messy Room Chemistry

Take a look around your room. Your bed takes up space and has weight. Chemistry is the study of your bed. What about your socks? They smell awful, right? That noxious odor can be studied by chemists. That two-week-old pizza under your bed? Yes, there's pretty nasty pizza chemistry going on down there. Chemistry is the air you breathe, the clothes you wear, the water you drink, and more!

But...

Chemists aren't simply interested in looking at your bed and the pizza that's under it. Anyone can do that. They want to understand what your bed and old pizza are made out of and how this stuff changes and interacts with other stuff. A chemist might take your bed out to the backyard and burn it. Your bed frame is interacting with the fire. Now, that's something worth studying (if you don't mind sleeping on the floor). Or a chemist might take that pizza to a lab and study how it has changed over time. A hungry chemist might head to the kitchen and make a new pizza, and study how yeast, flour, water, salt, and sugar make dough. That's edible chemistry. And, hey, if there's a large barrel of green radioactive slime oozing onto your bedroom floor, they'll study that, too.

All About This Book

Creating the *concoctions* in this book will give you an even better idea of what chemistry is about. You'll cause chemical *reactions,* create cool *solutions,* mix up chemical *compounds,* and more. Don't know what reactions, solutions, and compounds are? No problem. Simply turn to the glossary on page 76 and look up the words you don't understand. Anytime we mention a word that's in the glossary, we'll italicize it. After creating the concoction and amazing your friends and family, read **Why It Works,** for the chemistry behind the fun. The only other thing to know about this book, is that you need to read the next page before starting. It will make your chemistry experiments a lot more fun and safer to perform. Ready? Good.

Copy these lab rules and tack them up so you'll
always have them nearby.

Lab Rules

✔ Read each experiment all the way through before starting.
Then collect what you need and choose the spot that will serve as
your laboratory. You might work in the kitchen, the garage, or even
outdoors, but get an adult's permission for wherever you choose.

✔ If something unfamiliar is on a What You Need list, ask an
adult to help you find it. You might need to visit a drug store or a
supermarket.

✔ Don't use the substances for anything besides what is
instructed.

✔ Don't leave anything out where someone might mistake it
for a drink.

✔ Wash your hands very well.

✔ Use clean containers (jars, cups, glasses, bowls) for your
experiments. You can sometimes substitute containers or vary
their sizes.

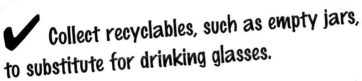 Collect recyclables, such as empty jars, to substitute for drinking glasses.

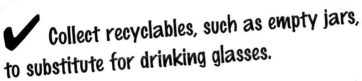 Clean all your materials after you use them and clean the area with paper towels and soap.

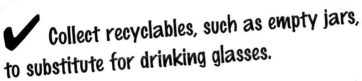 Never pour a polymer or slime concoction (pages 36, 38, 39, 40, 44, 45, and 57) down a drain. Always throw it away in the trash.

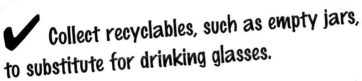 Get an adult to help you whenever there's a heat source involved, or anything using a flame or ammonia.

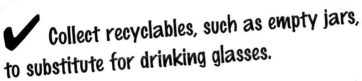 Always stop what you're doing and find an adult if you have questions or aren't sure what to do.

From Quite Small to Rather Large

Interested in the smallest things in the world—the stuff inside atoms? Then you are talking subatomic chemistry. How about stars, planets, and space itself? If you want to learn more about them you'll get into astrochemistry. Even if you think you aren't into science (maybe you just like animals or exploring outdoors or hanging out with your favorite people) you can't get away from chemistry. (Biochemistry is the study of the chemistry of people and other living things, including how chemicals make a living thing healthy or sick.) In fact, there are about as many kinds of chemistry out there as there are forms of matter to study.

Rock-My-World Candy

Chemistry isn't just incredible . . .
sometimes it's edible.

Crystal Lollipops

What You Need

Adult helper • Measuring cup • Water •
Saucepan • Stove • Sugar • Wooden spoon •
Small paper cups • Craft sticks • Plastic wrap

What You Do

Pour ½ cup of water into the saucepan. Slowly
sprinkle in 1 cup of sugar as you stir. Stop
adding sugar when it stops dissolving. Place the
saucepan on the stove and heat it on low heat for
two to three minutes, or until the sugar starts dissolving again. Add the rest of the sugar and cook the solution until all of the sugar dissolves, stirring it
occasionally. Then turn up the heat to medium-
high until the solution boils. Boil for one minute,
until the solution is thick and clear. Turn off
the heat and carefully pour the solution
into the cups. Stick one craft stick into
each cup, and cover loosely with
plastic wrap. Let your lollipops
sit undisturbed overnight. The lollipops will fully crystallize and
loosen from the sides of the
cups. (If they aren't ready,
let them set for another
24 hours.) You can
eat them.

Ahem.
Make sure an
adult is present
while using the
stove.

Candy Strings

What You Need

Adult helper • Glass jar • String • Skewer • Scissors • Measuring cup • Water • Sugar • Saucepan • Stove • Oven mitt • Candy thermometer • Wooden spoon • Aluminum foil

What You Do

Clean the jar well. Tie one end of the string to the skewer and cut it so it's long enough to hang down into the jar without touching the bottom when the skewer rests on top of the jar. Pour 2 cups of water and 5 cups of sugar into the saucepan. Place this concoction on a stove set at medium heat. Stir the mixture until it reaches 250°F, being careful not to let the thermometer touch the bottom of the saucepan. (It could get a false reading, or break from the heat.) Then turn off the stove. Pour the mixture into the jar. Cover the top of the jar loosely with aluminum foil. Wait overnight, and then gently begin pulling out the string: it should be covered with rock candy crystals. (If they aren't ready, release the string and let it set for another 24 hours.) You can eat it if you like.

Why They Work

Heating the water forces more sugar to dissolve than ordinarily could, leading to *supersaturation.* When the mixtures cool, the water can no longer hang onto all that extra sugar. So, after you pour the lollipop *solution* in the cups, the water *evaporates* and sugar *crystals* remain. When you make a candy string, sugar crystals form in the jar and on the string.

Cave Chemistry

Caves do chemistry all by themselves. And now, you too, can make your very own creepy cave rocksicles.

What You Need

Epsom salts • Water • Measuring cup • Bowl • Spoon • 2 short glasses • Ruler • Scissors • Cotton string • 2 large metal paper clips • Aluminum foil

What You Do

Find a workspace where you can leave your concoction undisturbed for a couple of days. Mix ⅔ cup Epsom salts and 1 cup very hot tap water in the bowl. Pour this solution into one glass. Cut a 10-inch length of string and tie a paper clip to each end. Then soak the string (paper clips included) in the solution for five minutes. Lay the aluminum foil on your work surface and set the glasses on top of the foil, approximately 5 inches apart. Pull one end of the string out of the solution and place the end into the empty glass. Make sure the string is a little slack. After about 30 minutes, check to see if you've grown any stalactites and stalagmites. (You should see some solution dripping from the string.) Check your creation again in an hour, a day, and even a couple of days.

14

Stalactites hang "tite" from the ceiling while stalagmites are on the ground.

Why It Works

Solids can dissolve in liquids, in which case the solid is a *solute*, the liquid is the *solvent,* and the product is a *solution*. (Water is known as the universal solvent, because more substances dissolve in it than any other liquid.) The higher the water temperature, the more solute *molecules* can be dissolved in the solvent. (When no more solute can dissolve, the solution is called *saturated*. Sometimes you get so much solute in it that it becomes *supersaturated*.) The water will *evaporate* (turn to *gas*) as it cools, but Epsom salts (*sulfates*) won't. So, as the solution drips from the string, the water evaporates and the sulfates are left behind and pile up and down. In caves, stalagmites and stalactites are formed in a very similar way, except instead of Epsom salts, the mineral deposited is often calcium carbonate or limestone.

15

Fossil-Making Fun

Tired of searching in vain for dinosaur fossils in your backyard? Well, whip up this simple concoction to make your very own old bones.

What You Need

Sponge • Scissors • Bowl • Sand • Measuring cups • Water • Pitcher • Table salt • Spoon • Trowel

What You Do

Cut the sponge into bones or other fossil shapes, place them in the bowl, and cover them with sand. Put a few cups of water in the pitcher, and then add table salt to the water as you stir. Add salt until the water is murky. Then pour the solution into the bowl of sand, drenching all the sand. Place the bowl in a sunny spot for a week, and then dig up the sponge fossils. If they're not stiff and dry, bury them again and let them set for another few days.

Why It Works

By making the saltwater murky, you're creating a *solution* that's *saturated* (soaked). That means no more of the *solute* (table salt) can dissolve in the *solvent* (water), so the excess floats around. When you pour this into the bowl, the sponge absorbs the saltwater and little bits of sand. The sponge keeps absorbing until it, too, is soaked full of the table salt. Sunlight heats the water, making the water *evaporate* (become a *gas*) quicker. Soon, all that's left is a sponge full of solid salt and sand.

Volcano

You don't need an earthquake to activate this volcano—household chemicals do the trick.

What You Need

Outdoor location • Tall bottle or jar • Modeling clay • White vinegar • Food coloring (optional) • Spoon • Baking soda

What You Do

Fill the bottle ½ full with the vinegar. Add three to five drops of red food coloring. Then sculpt the clay around the bottle, in the shape of a volcano, right up to the bottle's mouth. Sprinkle a heaping spoonful of baking soda in. Your concoction will fizz up and over the sides of the volcano like hot lava.

Why It Works

Vinegar is a *solution* of *acetic acid* in water. (Acetic acid is produced naturally when apples, grapes, and other fruit rot.) *Baking soda* is a *base*. When you mix an acid and a base, you get a *reaction*. How can you tell? Here, LOTS of bubbles form because the reaction created something new: *carbon dioxide* gas. The gas is *expanding*, and it fizzes right out of the bottle and down the sides of the clay volcano.

What Makes Your Pop POP?

In the 19th century, if you wanted a lemon-lime soda or a cola you wouldn't go to a grocery store. You'd stop at the local pharmacy. Why? Chemistry, of course...

Since ancient times, people have thought a soak in a natural spring heals or eases ailments—and that a sip is as good as a soak. Natural springs fill pools or streams with mineral water, which is a *solution* of dissolved salts, elements, or gases from the rocks and earth around it. Some mineral waters bubble. Curious chemists found that the bubbles were *carbon dioxide* gas, then experimented until they figured out how to get bubbles into regular water—creating their very own effervescent (carbonated) water.

How'd they do it? They created reactions to make the *gas*, including mixing *baking soda* with sulfuric acid—a scary-sounding liquid that's in lots of stuff, including fertilizer. Pumped into a *liquid*, the gas dissolves. But unless it's kept under pressure, such as in a tight-closing bottle, the gas bubbles until it's exhausted, and the drink goes "flat." No one knew how to keep the bubbles active, so carbonated water was made and sold to order at pharmacies. (It was considered a healthy drink, after all!)

Pharmacists—people trained like chemists to concoct and dispense medicines— added herbs and fruit extracts to the drinks. Each unique *concoction* improved health and tasted great, they said. They advertised soda pops for headache relief, to aid in digestion or cure stomach upsets, or to do vague things like invigorate and exhilarate. The drinks outsold the other medicines!

Did they work? Definitely maybe. Much of the "soda water" contained baking soda, which neutralizes *acids*, including stomach acids, potentially easing an upset stomach. Other common ingredients, such as caffeine and sugar, energize some folks, and might sidetrack a headache.

Then chemists invented a way to seal bottles, so people heard the pop sound of the gas as it escaped. Suddenly, "soda pop" could be sold and drunk anywhere.

Today, it would be hard to find anyone who says soda pop is good for you. But we can still thank those cola chemists for every sticky, sweet, bubbly sip!

Soda Slobber

This messy experiment makes ordinary cola foam at the mouth.

What You Need
Outdoor location • 2-liter bottle of cola (not diet) • *Funnel* • Tablespoon • Table salt

What You Do
Place the bottle in an outdoor location that you can easily clean (or leave a wet, sticky mess). Open the bottle and put the funnel in the bottle. Pour a tablespoon of salt in the funnel. Pull the funnel away and take a step back. Great foams of cola will bubble up and out and all over the place.

Why It Works
In *carbonated* beverages (soda pop, cola), *carbon dioxide* is dissolved in the drink. So we have a gas dissolved in a liquid that's bottled under *pressure.* Carbon dioxide happens to like to stick to solids. In this case, salt provides a solid surface for the gas bubbles to stick to. Pour the salt in, and the bubbles rush out.

Do-It-Itself Balloon

You'll say it looks like a trick, but an acid reaction (not magic) is at work.

What You Need

Small, clean empty bottle with a short neck • *Funnel* • White vinegar • Baking soda • Measuring spoons • Balloon

What You Do

Pour 4 tablespoons of vinegar into the bottle, and set it aside. Funnel a tablespoon of baking soda into a small balloon. Without spilling the baking soda, slip the mouth of the balloon onto the neck of the bottle. Now lift the balloon up so the baking soda falls into the vinegar. The concoction begins bubbling and the balloon will inflate.

Why It Works

The *baking soda* (a *compound* that is a *base*) and *vinegar* (a *solution* made with *acid* and water) *react,* forming *carbon dioxide.* This *gas* fills the bottle and has nowhere to go but up, up, up into the balloon.

Homemade Bubble Stuff

Use this concoction for super big bubbles that resist bursting.

What You Need

Empty ½ gallon milk carton, with lid • Water • Measuring cup • Liquid dish detergent • Measuring spoons • Glycerin (from a drugstore) • Shallow bowl • Bubble blower • Scissors

What You Do

Rinse out the milk carton and fill it with water, then pour out ⅓ cup of the water. Add ⅓ cup of the liquid dish detergent and 2 tablespoons of glycerin to the milk carton. Close it and slowly turn it over a couple times to mix it up. Don't shake it. Let it set for 24 hours. Then slowly pour some of the concoction into a shallow bowl. Dip the bubble blower in the solution, and blow. You'll make thick bubbles that float for a long time.

Why It Works

Water has a very high *surface tension* due to *hydrogen bonding* between its *molecules.* That means water gets a skin on its surface, explaining why water bugs can skitter across the surface. With water alone, the surface tension is too high for the bubble to last. (Try blowing a bubble made of pure water; it pops very quickly.) Adding soap puts detergent molecules between the water molecules, reducing the surface tension—allowing for bigger bubbles. Bubbles burst when the water evaporates, so adding glycerin makes bubbles last longer by slowing *evaporation.*

Bubble Business

The right concoction is the first step to getting bubbles to do backflips.

Bubble Acrobatics

What You Need

Outdoor location • A helper • Bubble concoction from page 21 • Large bowl • 4 feet of string • 4 straws • Bubble blower • Clean work surface

What You Do

Make the bubble concoction in the large bowl. Prepare to make a bubble "trampoline" by threading the string through the straws, end to end, making a square. Tie a knot where the string ends meet. Dip your square bubble trampoline in the bubble mixture so that it's got a film of bubble mixture. Have your helper hold it horizontally. Dip the bubble blower in the bubble mixture, pull it out, and gently blow a bubble toward the trampoline. Have your helper catch the bubble and bounce it on the filmy trampoline. She may need to practice. See how many times each of you can bounce a bubble before it breaks!

Why It Works

The bubble *solution* makes the bubbles strong enough to bounce on the "trampoline." (Read about it on the previous page.) Why are bubbles round, anyway? Bubbles form spheres because of *hydrogen bonding* that hold a bubble together. A sphere has the smallest surface area, so it is the preferred shape (as opposed to a cube or a hexagon, or other shape.)

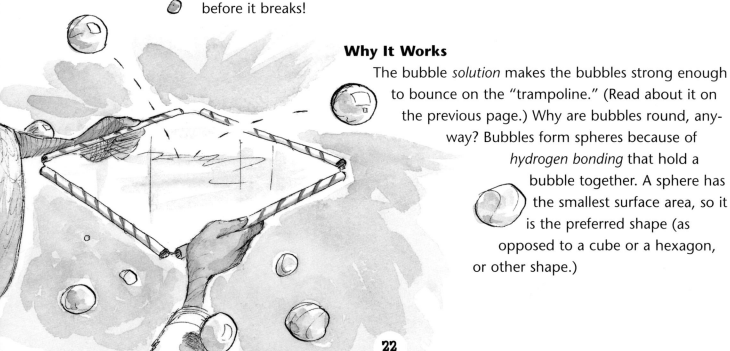

A Bubble that Bounces

What You Need

Water (distilled water works best) • Measuring cup • Liquid dish detergent • Measuring spoons • Glycerin (from a drugstore) or corn syrup • Bowl • Clean cotton gloves • Six-pack ring (from a six-pack of bottled or canned drinks) or bubble blower

What You Do

Combine 1 cup of water, 2 tablespoons of liquid dish detergent, and 1 tablespoon of glycerin in a bowl. Put on the cotton gloves. Dip the six-pack ring into the mixture, lift it out, and blow a bubble the size of a tennis ball. Let the bubble land on your gloved hand. It will bounce. (Try again if necessary. It works!)

Why It Works

Ordinary bubbles burst when they touch something. That's because dust, dirt, and oil attach to the surface of the bubble and break it. The combination of clean cotton gloves and glycerin or syrup in the bubble *solution* means that your bubbles are extra strong and the surface they contact (the gloves) are free of debris that would burst your bubbles.

In the Bag

You can see and feel this experiment working.

What You Need

Citric acid (found in health food stores) • Baking soda • Measuring spoons • Gallon-size resealable plastic bag • Sandwich-size resealable plastic bag • Water

What You Do

Put 1 tablespoon of citric acid and and 1 tablespoon of baking soda in the large bag. Fill the small bag halfway with room temperature water, leave it open, and put it inside the large bag. Seal the large bag. Shift the large bag so that you pour the water out of the small bag, mixing the water, baking soda, and citric acid in the large bag. You'll see the large bag inflate. Hold it and you can feel the water cool.

Why It Works

You've created a chemical *reaction*. The citric acid, baking soda, and water combine to create a new substance with a whole new chemical and physical form: *carbon dioxide* (as a *gas*) and water. The gas is *matter,* so it takes up space—and gases will expand indefinitely—so the bag must inflate. The reaction also absorbs heat from the water, making the water feel cooler. (There's actually no such thing as cold—there's just the absence of heat!)

Water Bomb

You'd never ever surprise someone with an exploding water bomb, right? Right.

What You Need

Outdoor location • Paper towel • Measuring spoons • Baking soda • Measuring cup • White vinegar • Water • Sandwich-size resealable plastic bag

What You Do

Tear a square of paper towel that's large enough to cover your out-stretched hand. Put 3 tablespoons of baking soda in the middle. Fold the paper towel around the baking soda, making a little packet. Then pour ¾ cup of vinegar and ¼ cup of warm water into the plastic bag. Drop the baking soda packet into the bag and quickly seal the top. You have a few seconds to put the bag somewhere before you watch it explode. (Don't get the concoction in your eyes—they'll sting until you rinse them.)

Why It Works

This is a variation of the classic baking soda (a *compound* that's a *base*) and vinegar (a *solution* that's an *acid*) *reaction*, which produces *carbon dioxide* (a *gas*). In this case, there's so much expanding gas in the bag that the pressure inside gets too great. The gas *molecules* pushing against the bag make it burst.

Head Shrinker

Make creepy shrunken heads from apples.

What You Need

2 fresh red apples • Knife • Epsom salts • 2 plastic cups (large enough to hold an apple) • Table salt • Marker

What You Do

Carve a face into each apple, leaving the skin on. Put one apple into each cup. Add enough Epsom salts to one cup to cover that apple and label that cup with an E. Cover the apple in the other cup with table salt. Label that cup with an S. Place the cups on a shelf out of direct sunlight and let them sit for seven days. Remove the apples from the cups. Compare and decide which compound (Epsom salts or table salt) produced the creepiest looking shrunken head.

Why It Works

Have you ever wondered why every time you eat salty foods, you get thirsty? The answer is simple: salt removes moisture. Salt is a *desiccant*—something that removes water from things, including human bodies and juicy apples.

Pass the Salt, Mummy!

Everyone has heard of mummies. You can probably picture one in your mind right now, even if you've never met one. That's because Egyptian mummies have lasted for millennia, all because ancient Egyptians knew their chemistry.

Preserving the body of a person who died was important to Egyptians. What they had to figure out was how to stop the natural chemical process of decomposition. Living things, such as plants and animals, are made up of *compounds* of carbon that decompose when they die. The process speeds up in the presence of water, because microbes live and reproduce in the moisture. So, when a tree falls in the forest, microbes make it decay into a pulpy mass and eventually sink into the forest floor as soil.

Egyptians used table salt as a spice, so they knew that it absorbed liquid and could dry living tissue (explaining the dry feeling in your mouth when you eat too much of it). Naturally occurring salts form when minerals from rocks dissolve in water. When the water *evaporates*, what you have left is the solid we call salt. It just so happens that the Nile River in Egypt contains a lot of dissolved salts. (When you evaporated the water, you got a salt.) Called natron, those salts were made up of sodium bicarbonate, sodium carbonate, sodium chloride, and sodium sulfate. It turns out that salt makes a human body inhospitable to microbes, so natron was a good choice for halting a body's decomposition.

Egyptians first removed the organs and liquids. Then they stuffed the body with pounds of natron. Since a body is up to 70 percent water, it needs a lot of drying. After a month or more, the chemical process ended and Egyptians removed the salts. While losing all that water to evaporation and absorption by the salts, body tissue shrinks and hardens. So, they cleaned the body, brushed it with oils and spices, and wrapped it in 20 layers of linen strips (to restore the shrunken body to the size and shape of the original person).

All you need to make a mummy is a lot of salt, and a strong stomach, and, um, a dead body. (Start with the apples on page 26.)

Crystal Garden

It's nothing short of amazing to see a patch of crystals sprout from this truly odd concoction.

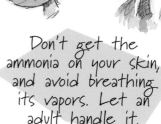

What You Need

Adult helper • Barbecue charcoal • Hammer • Fish bowl • Liquid fabric whitener (sold with cleaning supplies) • Measuring spoons • Water • Disposable cup • Table salt • Ammonia • Magnifying glass (optional) • Food coloring

Don't get the ammonia on your skin, and avoid breathing its vapors. Let an adult handle it.

What You Do

Hammer the charcoal into small chunks and place them in the fish bowl. Set it aside. Mix 7 tablespoons of fabric whitener plus 2 tablespoons of water in the cup. Now add 7 tablespoons of table salt and 1 tablespoon of ammonia to the concoction. Pour the concoction over the charcoal chunks. Set the fish bowl out of the way and observe it before you go to bed, and again the next day. (Use the magnifying glass to really see what's going on.) Crystals will start to form. Add color by dripping a few drops of food coloring onto the growing crystals.

Why It Works

True *solids* are made up of *molecules* with regular geometric patterns, such as a series of squares or triangles. These molecules are piled on top of one another, so the patterns are three-dimensional (raised), instead of flat (like a drawing). They are said to have *crystalline* shapes because crystals are clear and definite in form.

Giant Gems

With a little practice, this concoction will grow colossal crystals, like giant gemstones.

What You Need

Small container of alum (a pickling agent available in supermarkets) • Cup (larger than the alum container) • Water • Spoon • Jar • Dental floss • Pencil • Plastic wrap • Magnifying glass (optional)

What You Do

Make a solution by dissolving alum in very hot tap water. Do this by putting half of the alum in the cup, and stirring it constantly while slowly adding water until the mixture is very thick. Let this solution stand overnight, and then pour it into the jar. Alum crystals have formed at the bottom of the cup—tie them, one at time, onto one end of the floss. (Yes, this is hard to do.) Tie the other end of the floss to the pencil and hang the alum crystals in the jar of solution. Rest the pencil horizontally on the mouth of the jar. Cover it all loosely with plastic wrap (to keep dirt out) and put it in an out-of-the way place. After a week, you'll have several white gems that look like diamonds. Cut them away from the string and put them on display, or pick the best gem and grow it even more following the same instruction.

Why It Works

You *supersaturated* a *solution* and then let the water *evaporate* (like the projects on pages 12 to 15). Alum has a tendency to form *seed crystals* (small crystals that provide a base for further growth on their surfaces), and as long as you keep them in an alum solution, they will attract more alum molecules until all of the solution evaporates. That's how the crystal "grows."

Bendable Bones

You made a sponge into a bone (see page 16), now make a spongy bone.

What You Need
Chicken bones (cleaned by an adult)
• Large jar • White vinegar

What You Do
Put the clean chicken bones in the jar. Pour in enough vinegar to cover the bones, and then let the bones set for three days. Pour out the vinegar and remove the bones from the jar. You should be able to bend them any which way.

Why It Works
Bones are made of calcium and phosphorus *compounds.* Those minerals make bones hard and stiff. The *acetic acid* in the vinegar reacts with the minerals, dissolving them and leaving the remaining materials flexible.

Bouncing Egg

You can't bounce a raw egg—or can you?

What You Need

Egg • Glass or plastic container (wider and taller than the egg)
• White vinegar • Sink

What You Do

Put the egg in the glass. Put enough vinegar in the glass to cover the egg. Wait for 24 hours. Now observe the egg. The shell is gone. Remove the egg from the cup and drop it into the sink from 3 inches above. It will bounce. Continue dropping it from a greater distance each time, to see how high it will bounce before it splatters.

Why It Works

The egg bounces because the membrane becomes rubbery. This is due to osmosis, which is the flow of a *solvent* through semi-permeable membrane (a covering that allows some molecules to pass through, but not others) from one *solution* to another, less *concentrated* one. The rubbery membrane, plus the extra water in the egg that got there via osmosis, make it bounce. There's a limit to how much stress the membrane/egg will take though, so it will break eventually. (But where did the eggshell go? Read **Why It Works** on the next page to find out.)

Eggshell Eaters

When acids want to eat eggs, they order them hardboiled.

What You Need
Adult helper • Egg • Medium saucepan • Water • Stove • Tongs • Wax crayon • Clear glass (large enough to hold the egg) • White vinegar

What You Do
Boil the egg in the saucepan on the stove for 10 minutes. Turn off the stove, and use the tongs to remove the egg. Let it cool, and then use the crayon to write on the eggshell. (Write your name, write in Braille dots, or draw a design.) Place the egg in the glass and drown it in vinegar. You should see bubbles forming. Wait an hour, or until the bubbling stops. Carefully pour out the vinegar and replace it with fresh vinegar. Is it bubbling again? Wait another hour, or until the bubbling stops. Take the egg from the glass and rinse it under running water. Rub your fingers over the letters. You should feel what you wrote, but the rest of the eggshell has disappeared.

Why It Works
The eggshell doesn't dissolve, thought it looks as if it does. Vinegar is a *solution* of about 5% acetic acid in water. The *acid* reacts with a *base* substance—the *calcium carbonate* in the eggshell. This creates carbon dioxide and calcium acetate. The *carbon dioxide* is in the form of a *gas*; it makes the bubbles and escapes. The calcium acetate dissolves in the water. So, the eggshell disappears because it all reacted and formed new substances. Wax doesn't react to most acids, so the part of the eggshell under the wax crayon writing was protected.

Chemistry Crimestoppers

There's been a murder, but the detectives working the scene can't find any evidence to help them catch who did it. Instead of scratching their heads and saying, "Beats me," they call their forensic scientist. This scientist will analyze evidence already found using science (especially chemistry), and, if all goes as planned, find new evidence as well.

The forensic scientist arrives, surveys the scene, and decides to check for blood on a doorknob. He doesn't see any, but sprays a clear liquid called luminol on the knob. Suddenly the doorknob glows in a greenish-blue color. Someone, perhaps the killer, left blood residue on the knob. Luminol reacts so strongly to the components in blood, that it will glow even if the blood has been washed off.

Next, the forensic scientist finds a plastic bag by the door. The detectives haven't been able to get any fingerprints from the bag, but the scientist has a pretty nifty trick up his sleeve. He takes the bag back to his lab, puts it in a tent, and burns some cyanoacrylate glue (such as Krazy Glue). The chemical cyanoacrylate is attracted to the amino acids, fats, and proteins left behind by the finger, and forms a plastic mold of the print. Ta dah, fingerprint!

Thanks to forensic chemistry, crimes can now be solved with only a single carpet fiber as evidence. Or a fingernail. Even a single piece of hair, tested for its DNA can catch a crook. Want to be a crimestopping chemist, or a lab detective? Start by checking out the concoctions on pages 34 and 35.

Decode This!

Solve the mysteries of secret messages in the laboratory.

Outta-Sight Ink

What You Need
Half a lemon • Small bowl • Water • Cotton swab • Paper • Lamp with an incandescent (heat-producing) light bulb

What You Do
Squeeze the lemon juice into the bowl. Then add enough water to the lemon juice so that it's nearly colorless. Dip the cotton swab into the solution and write on the paper. Allow the paper to dry, and then hold it a few inches from the lamp and turn on the light. (Don't hold it too close to the bulb.) In a few seconds your writing will appear on the paper.

Why It Works
Lemon juice contains *citric acid.* Heat encourages the *acid* to *oxidize,* which is a chemical reaction between oxygen in the air and a substance. (Oxidation is what happens when you cut an apple and leave it sitting out: it turns brown because the citric acid in the apple oxidizes.) So when the lemon juice ink is heated by the lamp, the lemon juice turns brown. The writing appears!

Wrinkle-Free Ink

What You Need
Spray starch (used in ironing clothes) • Paper towels • Tincture of iodine (from a drug store) • Small spray bottle • Water

What You Do
Use the spray starch to write your initials or a simple messsage on a paper towel. (Keep it simple. The spray starch isn't easy to write with.) Drip one drop of the tincture of iodine in the spray bottle. Add enough water to dilute the iodine so that it resembles weak tea. Spray the iodine solution on the paper towel. Your writing will appear!

Freckle-Free Ink

What You Need

White-colored, high SPF sunblock • White scrap cloth • Paper towels • Dark room • Flashlight

What You Do

Squeeze out some sunblock into the palm of your hand. Dip your index finger in it and write in sunblock on the cloth. (Wipe the extra sunblock off your hands with the paper towels.) Grab the flashlight and take the cloth into a dark room. Shine the flashlight on the cloth. Your writing appears dark against the white fabric.

Why It Works

Sunblock is designed to absorb UV radiation (rays of sunlight that cause sunburns) so that it doesn't get to your skin and damage it. The sunblock also absorbs some visible light radiation (like light bulb light). So when you shine the flashlight, the sun block absorbs some of the light—making whatever you wrote appear darker than the fabric around it.

Why It Works

Starch is a type of sugar that's white or colorless. Cereal grains (oats, rye) and tubers (potatoes) have lots of starch. When starch comes in contact with iodine, they react and form a new material that's blue-gray. When you see something change color like that, it's a good bet you've made a chemical *reaction* and made something new.

Fistful of Slime!

Get you hands in a concoction that breaks the rules about what's a solid and what's a liquid.

What You Need
Bowl • Measuring cups • Water • Cornstarch • Food coloring (optional) • Resealable plastic bag

What You Do
Pour ⅓ cup of water into the bowl. If you want to add food coloring, drip five drops into the water. Measure ¾ cup of cornstarch and begin sprinkling it into the water, a little at a time, until the measuring cup is empty. Let the concoction stand for three or four minutes. Now reach a hand (or both!) into the concoction and press the slime into a hard ball. Open you hand and watch and feel the ball return to its liquid state! Store your slime in a resealable plastic bag. (Never pour slime down the drain. If you need to discard it, put it in the trash.)

Why It Works
Slime is a *polymer* (see **Poly-whats?,** page 37). It's also a non-Newtonian fluid. That means it breaks the rules that scientist Isaac Newton wrote saying a liquid moves and acts the same whether you're squeezing it, holding it, or just observing it. How does it do it? Cross-links of molecules and the right proportion of ingredients!

Poly-whats?

If you used a toothbrush, bounced a basketball, put on a raincoat, or ate ice cream today, did you remember to thank a chemist? They invented—or helped perfect—all those things by studying natural *polymers* and discovering how to make all the synthetic (manmade) ones you enjoy today.

Poly-whats?, you ask. Let us explain. Natural polymers are materials made up of long chains of identical molecules, called *monomers*. If you link a bunch of paper clips together, you've got a pretty good example of what these chains look like. (Each paper clip is a monomer.) These chains cross-link (attach to the other chains next to them) to form polymers. If you made a bunch of paper clip chains, jumbled them up, and threw them on a table, you'd have a polymer model. But the cross-link is nowhere near as strong as the links between the monomers in the polymer chains. (It's easier to separate the paper clip chains from each other than it is to separate each paper clip from its chain.)

Here's an example: Try to rip a plastic grocery bag. You'll notice that pulling it one way stretches the bag. You're pulling the polymer chains in the direction that they lay, so they stretch out. If you pull the other way, the bag will rip because you're pulling the polymer chains apart from the other chains where they aren't bonded together as well. If you rip a piece of newspaper a similar thing happens because newspaper is made of wood, a naturally occurring polymer. For a few examples of different types of polymers, check out **Fistful of Slime** (page 36), '**Snot for Everyone** (page 38), **Clean Green Slime** (page 39), **Bob the Bouncing Ball** (page 40-41), and **Moo-vable Milk** (page 57).

'Snot for Everyone

Everyone has boogers. But until now we bet you never had any you could share.

What You Need

Adult helper • Measuring cup • Bowl or saucepan • Water • Microwave oven or stove • 3 packages of unflavored gelatin • Food coloring • Spoon • Extra bowl • Light corn syrup • Resealable plastic bag

What You Do

Pour ½ cup water in the bowl (if you're using a microwave) or saucepan (if you're using a stove). Heat the water just until it boils, then remove the water from the heat source and turn it off. Sprinkle the gelatin in the water. Stir. If you want to add food coloring, do so now. Let the mixture sit for one minute. Measure the mixture as you move it to the extra bowl. Remember that amount, and add enough corn syrup to make 1 cup total in the bowl. Stir and lift out the long strands of snot you've made. If the snot thickens as it cools, add water spoonful by spoonful to thin it. Store your snot in a resealable plastic bag. (Never pour slime down the drain. If you need to discard it, put it in the trash.)

Why It Works

Water causes the gelatin *molecules* to *cross-link* and form a *polymer.* All polymers are made of many chains of identical molecules, connected by bridges called cross-links. So, lots of polymer/slime recipes will give you flexible, stretchable slime. But the corn syrup makes this slime especially snot-like.

Clean Green Slime

Think slime is too, uh, slimy? Try
making the cleanest slime there is.

What You Need
Adult helper • Warm water • Clean quart jar
with a lid • Measuring cup • Borax laundry
booster • Mixing bowl • Measuring spoons •
White craft glue • Green food coloring •
Resealable plastic bag

What You Do
Put 2 cups of warm water in the jar and add ⅛
cup borax. Close the lid and shake the jar until
the laundry booster dissolves. Allow the solution to cool. In the bowl, mix 1 tablespoon
of glue and 3 tablespoons of water. Add
2 drops of food coloring to the glue
mixture and stir well. Pour this mixture
into the bag. Now add 1 tablespoon of
the borax solution from the jar. Knead the contents of the bag.
You've got slime. Store it in the bag when you aren't testing how strong and stretchy it
is. (Never pour slime down the drain. If you need to discard it, put it in the trash.)

Why It Works
Slimes are *polymers:* chemical compounds formed by long chains of the same molecule.
Some polymers occur naturally (aloe plant juice) and some are manmade (chewing
gum). In Clean Green Slime, you create a polymer by mixing glue, borax, and water. The
glue is already a polymer, but it's very weak and sticky and would get full of dirt quickly if
you tried to play with it. For a better, cleaner polymer you make boric acid by dissolving
the borax soap (sodium borate) in the water, and then blend it with the glue.

Bob the Bouncing Blob

You don't have to name your blob Bob. It might be more of a Bill, or a Babette.

What You Need

Paper towels • 2 small plastic cups • Measuring spoons • White craft glue • Epsom salts • Water • Plastic spoon • Resealable plastic bag

What You Do

Cover your work surface with two layers of paper towels. Put 1 tablespoon of glue into one cup. Put ½ teaspoon of Epsom salt and ½ teaspoon of water in the other cup and mix that solution. Mix it some more. Did all the salts dissolve? It's okay if they didn't. Pour the solution into the cup of glue. Stir. Do you notice a change in the solution? Grab the glob you've made and pile it on your paper towel-covered work surface. Fold the towels over the glob and gently press the extra water out of it. Now discard the paper towels. Bend, twist, squeeze, and smoosh your glob. We also suggest rolling the glob into a round blob. Toss it at a clean, hard surface and try to catch it on the rebound. Store your blob in a resealable plastic bag. (Never pour a polymer concoction down the drain. If you need to discard it, put it in the trash.)

Why It Works

Glue remains a *compound* while making things stick together because it contains polyvinyl alcohol. That acts as a binder, keeping the glue semi-liquid and less likely to dry out. This makes glue perfect for making a *polymer*. The glue *cross-links* with the dissolved Epsom salts to create strong, flexible chains of molecules—which are characteristic of polymers. Roll them into a ball and they bounce!

Powder-Powered Projectile
(or, Pop Your Top)

Whatever you do, don't start this project and then poke your head real close to it to say "It's not working." That's asking for trouble.

What You Need

35mm film canister (it must have a ridge around the mouth of the canister to hold the lid on) • Water • Alka-Seltzer (an antacid and headache remedy)

What You Do

Fill the film canister half full of water. Break an Alka-Seltzer tablet in half, and put the half tablet in the film canister. Quickly put the lid on the canister. Stand back. Be patient. The top will fly up, up, and away.

Why It Works

Gases are made up of *particles.* How can you tell? If you swing a piece of paper through the air, you feel resistance. That's evidence of gas particles. When contained, say, in your bike tire, these particles exert *pressure.* Putting an Alka-Seltzer in water causes a *reaction* that makes *carbon dioxide* (a gas). It creates so much gas that the gas exerts pressure against all sides of the closed film container. The lid pops off because, compared to the sturdy walls and base, the lid offers the least resistance to the expanding gas.

Gas Power!

Gases don't get enough credit for all the work they do. (Maybe that's because they're usually invisible.) If you hold your breath, the longer you hold it in, the more pressure you'll feel inside your body. Your body removes oxygen from the air, because your bloodstream needs it, then releases a new concoction: carbon dioxide—enough to make the pages of this book flutter. Confining a gas to build pressure is part of the chemistry behind making things move forward, also known as propulsion. But to make things heavier than pages of a book move, you often need to create a chemical reaction as well. Then, just as you can launch the lid off the film canister on page 42 by creating a confined gas reaction, you can power a car, boat, train, or rocket.

All gases are made of particles that take up space. If you've shared a room with your brother or sister, you know there's only so much space in any given place. So, when room gets tight, the particles that exert the most force get their way and get as much room as they need. Objects generally can't move themselves around, so if the object's mass is greater than that of the gases, it will just stay put. But gases move around quite a bit. Expanding gases are powerful gases. They are often created by chemical reactions and have momentum—mass and velocity (speed). These gases make other gases and objects move out of their way.

In cars, fumes from gasoline ignite, releasing an enormous amount of energy, making the engine run. On ships and trains with steam engines, water is boiled to create steam. The gas is contained so that it builds up enough pressure to make the turbines turn and propel the ship or train forward. Rockets burn fuel in a small area, creating the fiery mass of released gas that you see below a launching rocket.

So now you know that gases are not just keeping you alive, but helping you move around the world. Did you thank them?

Disappearing Acts

These activities are all about destroying ugly ties and dorky sleepwear, packing peanuts, and foam cups. (Get an adult's permission first.)

Dispose of this noxious concoction by absorbing the liquid with paper towels. Place the soggy towels in the trash.

Tie Be Gone

What You Need

Adult helper • Nail polish remover (with acetone) • Glass or ceramic bowl (not plastic) • Old tie, nightgown, or underwear made of acetate (read the label)

What You Do

Pour half of the bottle of nail polish remover in the bowl. Dip the clothing into the bowl, and then pull it out and look at it. Repeat. The nail polish devours the clothing. Don't worry, it can't eat your fingers. But it might turn them white, temporarily.

Why It Works

Acetate (the material in the article of clothing you destroyed) is a *polymer,* which means it's made up of *monomers* (single long chains of identical *molecules*). *Acetone* (the main ingredient of the nail polish remover) breaks the chains. It looks as if the acetate disappears, but the un-linked molecules are floating in the acetone.

44

Who Ate My Peanuts?

What You Need
Packing peanut (starch-based, not polystyrene, available at mail centers) • Cup • Water

What You Do
Place one packing peanut in the clear cup. Fill the cup with water. Wait half an hour, and then look in the cup. The packing peanut has disappeared. Or has it?

H_2O

Get away, I'm a starch-based peanut!

Hug!

Shrivel

What You Need
Foam cup (polystyrene-based) • Platter • Rubbing alcohol

What You Do
Place the cup on the platter. Pour in a splash of rubbing alcohol. The cup starts shriveling up!

Why They Work
Packing peanuts are *polymers.* Some polymers can be dissolved by *solvents,* like the acetate tie that dissolves in the acetone on page 44. *Starch*-based polymers dissolve in water, so it looks as if the starch peanuts disappear, when really you've made a starch *solution.* Polystyrene-based polymers dissolve in *alcohol.* (In the process, dissolving breaks the cross-links that define polymers.) Why do these polymers dissolve so easily? They are full of *gas.* In the case of packing peanuts, they are only 5% solid. The other 95% is *carbon dioxide* (a gas). It's used to puff the peanuts into shape.

Color Change Tricks

A leopard can't change its spots, but you can change the color of a concoction with a few of the right drops. Drink the tea if you dare!

Terrible Tea

What You Need

Adult helper • Cup • Water • Microwave, or stove and saucepan • Teabag of black (caffeinated) tea • Lemon • Cutting board • Knife

> Give it to me. I'll try anything!

What You Do

Make the tea by placing the teabag in very hot (nearly boiling) water and letting the tea steep. (That means soak it in the hot water to extract the tea flavor and color from the teabag). Note the color of the tea. Then cut the lemon into quarters and squeeze lemon juice into the tea. The tea color will fade. How much lemon do you need before the tea color fades?

Why It Works

Lemons contain *citric acid.* That chemical and the dye in the tea (called tannin), undergo a *reaction.* The dye is bleached. Bye-bye black tea color!

Wacky Water

What You Need

Adult helper • Water • Measuring cup • Small saucepan • Oven mitt • Stove • Cornstarch •
Measuring spoons • Mixing spoon • 3% hydrogen peroxide • White vinegar • Tincture of iodine •
• Drinking glass • Medicine dropper • Baking powder

What You Do

Heat 1 cup of water in the saucepan over medium heat, mixing in 1 teaspoon of cornstarch until it
dissolves. Remove the pan from the heat and add 1 more cup of water, ½ cup of hydrogen peroxide, and 5 drops of vinegar. Stir. Add 2 drops of tincture of iodine to the bottom of the glass, and
then pour the solution from the pan into the glass. Watch the solution change from clear to blue.
Sprinkle in 1 teaspoon of baking powder. Wait a few seconds. The solution turns back to clear.

Why It Works

This is an example of what chemists call a clock reaction. We saw in **Wrinkle-Free Ink** (page 34)
that *starch* turns blue in the presence of iodine. In this *reaction,* you also have hydrogen peroxide
and *vinegar.* Their reaction affects how much and when the
iodine reacts with the starch in this experiment. (The
iodine does end up turning the starch blue.) Adding
the *baking powder* demonstrates a reversible reaction—
one that can go backwards. So, the starch turned blue
(forward reaction), and then turned back
(reverse reaction).

I can
do that!

Color Chromatography

Break colors down to their chemical components for a peek inside what makes a color a color.

Awash with Water

What You Need

Stain-resistant work surface • Paper coffee filters • *Medicine dropper* • Red food coloring • Blue food coloring • Toothpick • Water

What You Do

Lay a coffee filter on your work surface. Add 1 drop of red onto it. Then add 1 drop of blue. Stir the color with the toothpick. You've created purple. Now drip 1 or more drops of water on the color and wait for one minute. You'll see several different colors—shades of red, blue, and purple—from the color you made.

Not-So-Permanent Markers

What You Need

Stain-resistant work surface • Paper coffee filters • Brown and black permanent markers (other markers work, but not as well) • *Medicine dropper* • Rubbing alcohol • Cup • Water

What You Do

Lay out two coffee filters on your stain-resistant work surface. Pick a marker and make a pea-sized dot on one coffee filter. Do the same with the other marker, on the other coffee filter. Use the medicine dropper to drip alcohol on each dot, one drop at a time, until the color separates. You'll see that the each dot separates into several colors.

Why They Work

Water is a *solvent,* meaning it can dissolve another substance. (Substances that dissolve in water are called *hydrophilic.*) Water dissolves the food coloring, so the water goes into the coffee filter but the basic color stays on the top. But the colors in permanent markers are *hydrophobic,* meaning they are not soluble in water. So, even though water is a solvent for food coloring, it won't have an effect on permanent markers. That's why you used the *alcohol,* to achieve the same effect.

Super Suds

There's a fine line between super suds and bubble trouble. Good luck!

What You Need

Outdoor location • Liquid dish detergent • Tall plastic cup (or other containers of your choice) • Warm water • Measuring cups • Baking soda • Citric acid (available at health food stores)

What You Do

Work outdoors, or in an easy-to-clean location. Mix 3 big squirts of liquid dish detergent, ½ cup of warm tap water, and 1 heaping teaspoon of baking soda in the cup. Sprinkle two pinches of citric acid into the solution. Stand back, unless you want to be splattered with foam! (You can adjust these quantities to the size of your container as needed, or to experiment at making more foam.)

Why It Works

Baking soda is a *base.* When you add *acid,* it produces carbonic acid. This newly formed acid breaks down into water and *carbon dioxide,* as a *gas.* The gas launches the bubbles.

Sudsational Chemistry

Back before there were hundreds of soaps to choose from at the grocery store—heck, back before there were grocery stores—soap was made from animal fat (yuck!) and wood ashes. The fat had to be removed from a dead animal and cooked until it was liquid. The wood had to be burned until it was reduced to ashes, and then the ashes were thrown in the liquefied fat. While cooling, the concoction would become solid. Then you had soap.

People making this soap probably didn't know why the soap worked—but they knew it did. It wasn't until the 1800s that chemists could explain that salt *alkalis* in the *sodium carbonate* in the ashes *bonded* with the fat. So, if you rubbed your hands with this soap, the salt would rub off any dirt it touched, and the dirt would stick to the fat. If you then rinsed your hands with water, the fat and dirt washed away.

That's how soap was made for thousands of years: at a campfire or in a kitchen, using some combination of a surfactant (dirt remover) and a suspension (what carries the dirt). People varied the strength of soap concoctions (mild for hair washing, strong for cleaning pots and pans). They also made it as a solid, liquid, paste, or powder, depending on its intended use. Not only was soapmaking difficult, it was often very time-consuming. Hence, lots of people didn't (or couldn't) bother with it. They'd just rinse themselves and their belongings in water. (Which sure didn't help stop the spread of the plague and other epidemics that killed millions of people.)

In 1791 a French chemist figured out how to get sodium carbonate from *table salt*, and stop using wood ash. Suddenly, soap could be made easier, cheaper, and cleaner. It was made in huge batches and was sold cheaply to anyone who wanted it. Thankfully, the world became a cleaner place.

Crush Me If You Can

You've made concoctions explode. Can you make one implode? (Read more to find out what that means!)

What You Need

Adult helper • Ice • Water • Bowl • Saucepan • Stove • Empty aluminum soda can • Tongs

What You Do

You are going to put water in the saucepan, bowl, and aluminum can. Here's the order we suggest: Fill the bowl one-half full of ice, and then add enough cool water to cover the ice. Set the bowl near the stove. Fill the saucepan ¾ full of water and heat it on high. As the water in the saucepan warms to a boil, put just enough water inside the aluminum can to cover its bottom. Now is the time to exercise caution: When the water is boiling, use the tongs to grab the aluminum can and hold it right-side up in the boiling water. When a steady stream of steam comes from the can's opening, quickly remove the can from the boiling water and in the same motion turn it upside-down and dunk the can's opening into the bowl of water. The can crushes itself! (Don't forget to turn off the stove.)

Flip

Why It Works

The *pressure* of a *gas* and its *temperature* are directly related. If you heat up a gas, you increase the pressure (and *volume*). (That's why some aerosol cans warn that the "contents are under pressure" and advise keeping them "away from heat.") In this activity, heating the water to boiling changes it to a gas. Plunging the can (hole down) into ice water rapidly decreases the temperature. And you just learned that that means the pressure must also decrease quickly. Nature likes *equilibrium*—for things to be equal. So, to make the pressures inside and outside the can equal, the can implodes (collapses inwardly with great force).

Here's a new way to compact your recyclable soda cans.

53

Lava Lamps

Make these groovy self-contained chemical experiments and get a new handle on what it means to be dense.

Sphere Scene

What You Need
Clear bottle with a lid • Vegetable oil • Water • Food coloring

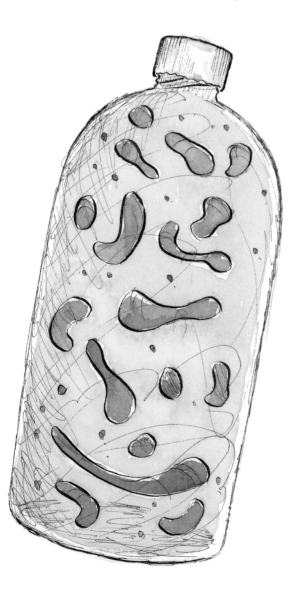

What You Do
Fill the bottle ¾ full with vegetable oil. Add water to the bottle, until it's almost full. Add 5 drops of food coloring. Put the lid on tight and turn the bottle on its side or upside-down. The water and oil will move around until the denser liquid—the colored water—settles on the bottom.

Why It Works
Density is determined by dividing a material's volume (how much space it takes up) by its mass (how much it weighs). Another way to judge something's density is by relating it to other materials: things that are less dense float on top of things that are more dense. That's why whipped cream floats on hot chocolate. Since oil is less dense than water, the oil will float on top of the water if you hold the bottle sideways. Here's a trick: shake it up and the colored water will form spheres inside the oil. That's because there's three times more oil than water in the bottle.

Ocean of Motion

What You Need

Clear bottle with lid • Vegetable oil • Water • Food coloring • Antacid tablet (Alka-Seltzer brand works best)

What You Do

Fill the bottle ¾ full of vegetable oil. Add water until the bottle is almost full. Then add 5 drops of food coloring into the bottle. Now break the antacid tablet into tiny pieces. Drop one small piece into the bottle and watch what happens. When it stops bubbling and the globules stop moving around, add another tablet piece. Put the cap on the bottle if you want to store your concoction.

Why It Works

Instead of shaking the bottle, the antacid tablet does the work for you. The antacid (which means against acid) is made to *react* with the acids in your stomach, but here it reacts with the water to form bubbles of *carbon dioxide* (as a *gas*). The gas bubbles are less dense than the water, so they rise. The gas bubbles will carry some water up with them, too. Eventually the bubbles burst, so the water sinks back down to the bottom of the bottle. The motion continues until the tablet is used up by the reaction.

Suspended Animation

Will it float, sink, or swim? Find out by dropping it in this carefully crafted concoction.

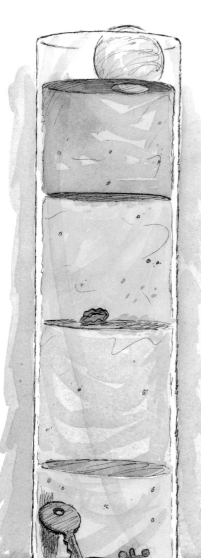

What You Need

Clear jar • Corn syrup or honey • Water • Cooking oil • Rubbing alcohol • Measuring cups (optional) • Spoon • Key, jack, and/or paper clip • Raisin, half a peanut, noodle, piece of cereal, and/or staple • Very small balls, such as a ping pong ball and rubber bouncing balls

What You Do

Fill the container ¼ full of each liquid, in the following order: corn syrup, water, cooking oil, alcohol. It's crucial that you don't disturb the layers below when adding the next liquid. Pour very slowly onto the back of the spoon and let the liquid go gently into the container. If some of the liquids mix, let the concoction set for a minute so the liquids can separate. Carefully, gently drop the key into the middle of the container. Gently drop in other objects, one at a time. They'll float, sink, or swim at different levels.

Why It Works

We know things that are less *dense* float on top of things that are more dense. If you can do this *concoction* carefully enough, you will see layers. Corn syrup is the most dense, so it sinks to the very bottom. Water is less dense, so it will float on top of the corn syrup. Cooking oil is even less dense, so it floats on top of the water. And the *alcohol* is the least dense, so it floats at the very top. The *density* and *mass* of objects you drop in vary. So where they rest depends on how those characteristics relate to each liquid's density.

Moo-vable Milk

You'll be udderly fascinated when you transform milk into a plastic!

What You Need

Adult helper • Measuring cup • Skim milk • Microwave-safe bowl • White vinegar • Measuring spoons • Microwave • Sieve • Sink • Airtight container

What You Do

Pour 1½ cups of skim milk in the bowl, and then add 4 teaspoons of vinegar. Microwave the concoction on high for 1 minute. Observe the concoction: it should have separated into a liquid and a solid. Stir the concoction, and then pour it through the sieve. (Do this over a sink, so you don't make a mess.) You'll have a plastic-like glob of milk rubber in the sieve that you can shape any which way. Let it cool and rinse it lightly before handling it. Store it in an airtight container. (Never put a polymer concoction down the drain. When you are ready to dispose of it, put in a trash can.)

Why It Works

Vinegar is an *acid*. (So it tastes sour.) Though milk contains some acid, it's primarily a *base*. When acids and bases mix, both change. The first result you notice here is that the milk fat becomes solid and the milk whey becomes a thinner liquid. The other result you notice when you shape the milk rubber: it feels and acts like *plastic*. It has become a *polymer*. The vinegar reacted with the proteins in the milk fat, causing them to *cross-link* to form long chains of *molecules*. So your milk rubber is a plastic at heart!

57

Geyser

Get ready to send a jet of soda pop right in the air!

What You Need

Outdoor location (or kitchen towels and an easy-to-cleanup space) • Unopened 2-liter bottle of soda (not diet) • Wintergreen Lifesavers • Drinking straw • Umbrella (optional)

What You Do

Do this activity outdoors where you won't have to clean up. Open the 2-liter bottle and set it on the ground in the center of your location. Unwrap the package of Wintergreen Lifesavers and put the drinking straw through their centers. Carefully place one end of the straw in the mouth of the bottle and pour in all the mints at once. Run away or prepare to get wet, because the contents of the bottle will shoot several feet into the air.

Why It Works

Carbonated drinks have *carbon dioxide* (a *gas*) dissolved in them. The gas makes them bubbly. (That gas is what makes you burp after drinking a bubbly drink.) The drinks are bottled under high *pressure,* because gas normally takes up space but you don't want to have more gas than drink in the bottle. When you open the bottle and hear the fizzing sound, that's the gas escaping into an area of low pressure (the air outside of the botte). When you drop in the breath mints, you provide a surface for the carbon dioxide to *react* with—and the result is soda rushing out of the bottle.

Spouting Off

A geyser is a natural spring that hurls a jet of hot water and steam into the air. Geysers can also bubble and burp up, be surrounded by colorful boiling pools, and, quite frankly, stink. Chemistry controls the spectacular sights, sounds, and smells of geysers—and most of it happens underground.

Geysers exist wherever there are underground pockets of water and molten (so hot it glows) rock. In the 1840s a German chemist, R. W. Bunsen, developed a theory for how geysers work. Bunsen's studies were done above ground, since it's hard for a person to survive in molten rock and boiling hot water. He visited the most famous geyser of the time, Geysir, in Iceland. Geysir still shoots 360 feet in the air, and it was so remarkable and unusual at the time that all other geysers were named after it.

Here's what Bunsen discovered: Rainwater fills underground springs. The water acts as a *solvent*, dissolving *elements* and *compounds* from nearby rocks and dirt, such as sulfur, iron, arsenic, and silica. Meanwhile, the heat from the rock increases the temperature of the water. Water expands when it's heated, which makes the water trapped underground take up more room. The expansion of the water creates pressure underground. This makes the pressure underground build. Nature seeks equilibrium—a state of all things being equal or in balance—so the pressure wants to be released. Eventually the pressure gets so high that the moment some of the water becomes steam (a gas), the underground pocket can no longer contain the whole concoction—so it's ejected into the air.

Since this water is boiling hot, you don't want to be too close when it shoots out. Some geysers erupt on a regular schedule; others erupt randomly—so you may not have any warning. (Yellowstone National Park in the United States is famous for its geysers. That's where you'll find Old Faithful, which, as you can tell by its name, erupts at regular intervals—about once an hour.)

After the showy display, much of the water evaporates and the rest of the *solution* pools nearby. Sulfur creates a rotten-egg smell and is yellow; iron oxidizes and turns reddish; arsenic is orange; silica is blue. The geyser looks calm after spouting off, but the chemical process is already beginning again underground.

Paint Party

Our experiments with chalk, milk, eggs, and cold cream demonstrate that scientists have an artistic side!

In Your Face

What You Need

Cornstarch • Water • Cold cream • Measuring spoons • Small bowl • Food coloring • Fork • Airtight container

What You Do

Measure 2 teaspoons of corn starch and a teaspoon each of water and cold cream into the bowl. Add 3 drops of food coloring. Thoroughly mix the concoction with a fork until it's the consistency of a very thick pudding. You have face paint! (You can also use it on washable surfaces.) Store it in an airtight container between uses.

Milk It

What You Need

1 cup condensed milk • Medium-sized bowl • Food coloring

What You Do

If you want to make several different colors, pour a little milk into several small bowls, and then add color to each bowl. To make just one color, pour all the condensed milk into the medium-sized bowl and add 4 drops drops of food coloring. Ta-dah! You've got shiny, bright paint. Use with permission and avoid staining your clothes.

Scrambled (Hold the Toast)

What You Need
Easy-to-clean work surface • Egg • Small bowl • Water • Spoon • Fork • Food coloring

What You Do
Crack the egg and put the yolk in the bowl. (Discard the egg white and eggshell.) Add 10 drops of food coloring and a spoonful of water into the bowl. Thoroughly blend the concoction with a fork, adding water as needed to achieve a paint-like consistency. You'll have a high-gloss color to paint with. (This paint washes off fairly easily, so IF you have permission, paint with it in the bathtub, on a countertop, or on paper. It can stain your clothes.) Don't store this paint—throw away what you don't use.

Chalk It Up

What You Need
Colored chalk • Hammer • Bowl • Spoon • Measuring cups • Water • White glue

What You Do
Crush the chalk until you have a fine powder. Move the chalk dust to a bowl. For every two sticks of chalk you smashed up, add 1 tablespoon of white glue and ¼ cup of water. Use the spoon to mix it well. You just made paint. When you use it, it will dry to a glossy finish. This paint doesn't come off easily, so only use it in art projects. Store it in an airtight container between uses.

Why They Work
Sometimes things we think might be *solutions* actually aren't. There are some technical distinctions. In a true solution, the *particles* are very small and we can't see them. In a *colloid* the particles are bigger, but we still can't see them. In a suspension, the particles are big enough to settle out. Paint is a suspension. If you open a can of paint that's been sitting for a while you will see a layer of oil or water at the top because the paint pigment particles have settled out. So you have to stir the paint really well before you use it.

Fountain Fun

Make water defy gravity as you turn it from liquid to gas.

What You Need

Adult helper • Awl • Cork (that fits in the glass bottle) • Scissors • Tube • Glass bottle • Clear glass • Water • Stove (gas range works best) • Food coloring

What You Do

First you need to prepare the route the water will take as it squirts up like a fountain. Do this by using the awl to make a hole through the cork that is just large enough to fit the tube through. (The fit needs to be snug.) Then invert the bottle over the glass and determine how much tube you need reach from the bottom of the glass into the bottle's neck. Cut that length of tube, put one end of the tube through the cork, and set this aside. Now put two drops of water in the bottle. Fill the glass ¾ full of water and add a drop of food coloring to it. Using tongs or an oven mitt to hold the bottle, heat water over the stove on medium. (If using a gas stove with a flame, you can heat on the lowest setting that creates a flame.) Do not touch the bottle to the heating element. When you see steam rise from the bottle, immediately put the cork and tube in the bottle—letting the long end of the tube hang out—and invert the bottle over the glass of water, placing the tube in the water. Watch the water fly up into the bottle.

Why It Works

Heating water to boiling causes a *gas* to form. When inverted, cooling occurs in the flask. Thus the decrease in *temperature* means a decrease in *pressure* inside the flask. Nature seeks *equilibrium*—for things to be equal. Since the cork and tubing stop air from getting into the flask, a partial *vacuum* is created and the water is sucked up into the flask.

Full of Hot Air

Invisible forces make a balloon do the opposite of what everyone expects. (Hint: there's no up, up, up!)

What You Need

Large bowl • Ice water • Empty plastic bottle • Water • Balloon

What You Do

Fill the bowl with ice water. Set it aside as you fill the bottle with very hot tap water and swish it around to heat up the bottle. Then pour out the water and refill the bottle ¼ full with very hot tap water. Place the mouth of the balloon over the neck of the bottle and stand up the bottle in the bowl. Watch the balloon get sucked into the bottle! (For quicker results, boil the water—in which case you'll need an adult helper.)

Why It Works

The *temperature* and *volume* of a *gas* are directly related. When air heats up, it expands; cool air contracts. When you first place the balloon over the bottle, the air in the bottle is hot. As the ice water cools the air, the air contracts and tries to pull more air in from the outside. The balloon is sucked into the bottle.

Indication Chemistry
(or, You Can't Hide)

Make a concoction and use it to create chemical reactions that reveal the essential nature of various ingredients.

Color-Coded Cabbage

What You Need

Adult helper • Apron or lab coat (cabbage juice stains!) • ¼ head of red cabbage • Cutting board • Knife • Blender • Water • Sieve • Jar

What You Do

Chop the red cabbage with the knife on the cutting board. Put the cabbage in the blender and add enough water to cover the vegetable pieces. Blend for a minute, or until the water is uniformly purple. Pour the contents of the blender through the sieve so that the juice winds up in the jar or bowl. (Do this over the sink to avoid a big mess.) You have made a purplish liquid that will be your indicator for the experiment on the next page.

Never let a kid operate a blender without reading the manual first!

Why It Works

How *acidic* or *basic* something is can be determined by using an *indicator.* You may have seen lifeguards at the pool testing the acidity of the water by putting some water into a vial and shaking it up. The indicator makes the water turn a color, and they then compare the color to a standard that tells whether or not it's okay to swim in. Here you'll use red cabbage juice as an indicator. Red cabbage contains *anthocyanins,* a *water-soluble* pigment that changes color depending on whether something is an acid or a base. So you can use it to determine if something is acidic or basic, depending on what color the cabbage juice turns when you add the material in question.

Acid or Base?

What You Need

Cabbage juice from page 64 • Measuring cup • Clear glass • White vinegar • Baking soda • Baking powder • Measuring spoons

What You Do

Measure ¼ cup of purple cabbage juice and pour it in the glass. Now measure out an equal amount of vinegar and pour it in the glass of cabbage juice. The concoction turns pinkish red. Measure ¼ teaspoon of baking soda and sprinkle it into the red concoction. It turns bluish green. Measure ¼ teaspoon of baking powder and sprinkle it into the bluish-green concoction. The purplish color returns!

Why It Works

Cabbage juice is an *indicator* because it changes color as it reacts with acids and *bases.* You made the *reaction* by adding vinegar (an acid) to the cabbage juice. The result was that the vinegar bleached it, and the purplish color became pinkish red. (See another example of acid's bleaching effect in Terrible Tea on page 46.) You made another *reaction* by adding baking soda to the concoction. The concoction turned bluish green. Why did the cabbage color come back? You *neutralized* the acid by adding the baking powder (a base) to the concoction. Neutralizing undoes the effect of the acid reaction. (The concoction is now completely neutral—it's neither an acid nor a base.) Make more cabbage juice and test to discover the nature of other substances!

Doubling Dough Balls

This concoction rises to the occasion.

What You Need

Adult helper • Flour • Measuring spoons •
Quick-rising dry yeast (found in grocery stores)
• Small bowl • Fork • Water • Spoon
• Ceramic or glass cup •
Aluminum foil

What You Do

Mix 1 tablespoon of flour and ½ teaspoon of yeast in the bowl. (Use these proportions for each dough ball you make.) Spoon just enough water into the bowl to create a dough ball about the size of a walnut. (If it gets too wet, add flour until you can roll a solid ball.) Set the dough ball aside on a piece of aluminum foil. Fill the cup with boiling water. Now hold the aluminum foil by its edges and hold the dough ball over the cup of boiling water. After about two minutes your dough ball will double or triple in size.

Why It Works

A *solid* isn't always so solid—some of what makes it take shape are *gases* inside it. Combining yeast, flour, and water makes a dough ball—you can see and feel that. But when you add heat to the *concoction,* you cause a *reaction* that produces invisible *carbon dioxide* (a *gas*). Gas is *matter,* so it takes up space, and likes to expand. It pushes the solid *molecules* around to make room for itself, inflating the dough ball.

Cupcake Chemistry

Cooking is chemistry. The kind of cooking we call baking has the most interesting (and tasty) chemical reactions: cakes and breads rise (or fall!), cookies and pastries brown (or burn).

From mixing the batter to getting it in the oven, you're preparing edible chemical *compounds*. Carbon, nitrogen, oxygen, hydrogen—it's all in there, and more.

Cupcakes are supposed to be moist and light, and to be completely cooked but not burnt. To achieve this ideal, you have to get the chemical process right when you select your ingredients, mix them, and heat the cupcakes.

The first thing a cupcake recipe will tell you to do is turn the oven on. The heat will cause *carbon dioxide* (a *gas*) to expand when you bake the cupcakes (which means fluffy delicious cupcakes). But how does the carbon dioxide get in there? It's not on the ingredients list…

When you make the batter, a *concoction* that is semi-liquid, you are blending flour, sugar, table salt, and baking soda with water, oil, vinegar or eggs, and vanilla. To be moist and light, cupcakes need an *alkali* and *acid* reaction to create carbon dioxide bubbles in the batter. Baking soda will react a little bit when mixed with any liquid, making the carbon dioxide. You can give the baking soda an additional power boost by combining it with vinegar or egg. This will make your cupcakes rise more.

The batter's starches, sugars, and proteins undergo chemical changes due to the heat, which is good if you like a cooked cupcake. When the starches have had as much heat as they can take, they release carbon *molecules*. The carbon turns brown, letting you know your cupcake is done. If you leave the cupcake in the oven, the carbon will turn black. The longer it's exposed to the heat, the more the cupcake releases carbons and turns brown or black.

So don't forget that your kitchen is your other laboratory. Use it to make delicious concoctions!

Float This

The simplest concoction is all you need to make you think twice about what floats and what doesn't.

I see my eggs are being put to good use.

What You Need

2 clear glasses • Water • 2 eggs
• Table salt • Measuring spoon

What You Do

Fill one glass halfway with water and carefully place one egg in it. The egg will rest on the bottom of the glass. (Of course it does! An egg is heavy!) Fill the other glass halfway with water, add 10 tablespoons of salt, and then carefully place the egg in the concoction. The egg will float. If you add more salt, does the egg float higher?

Forget about eggs! Try this experiment with people!

Why It Works

You can change the *density* of a substance by heating it, cooling it, or adding something to it. You can test a substance's density by putting something in it and noting how much buoyancy (upward lift) the test item has. Here you test the density of water as a liquid. The density of plain drinking water is low. *Salt* is a *desiccant*, which means it absorbs water. So, when you put the it in the water, its *molecules* become bloated with water molecules and sink, creating a highly *dense* layer of saltwater. The egg floats! This experiment also works with people, but you'll need a lot of salt. (Try the ocean!)

Rust in Peace

You need a few days and an observation space to create this chemical reaction.

What You Need

Steel wool (used for cleaning, without a detergent coating) • Water • Jar (make sure its base is not larger than the steel wool, but that you can reach into it) • Shallow bowl with a flat bottom, larger than the mouth of the jar

What You Do

Get the steel wool soaking wet. Place it in the bottom of the jar. You want a tight fit so it won't fall down when you invert the jar. Turn the jar upside down in the shallow bowl. Set the bowl and jar in a place where they won't be disturbed, then fill the bowl witih water. Observe the steel wool daily, replenishing the water in the bowl as needed. The steel wool will sprout red growth (rust!) and the water will fill the jar.

Why It Works

Steel wool is made of an *element* called *iron*. Being in an airtight container with lots of moisture (the water) encourages the iron to react with *oxygen* in a process called *oxidation*. The result is ferric oxide: rust. Rust is the reddish-brown coating that forms on the surfaces of iron when the metal is exposed to air and moisture. Why is the water level rising? When the iron and oxygen react, they form a new substance. The oxygen is used up, so there's more room in the jar for the water to move in.

My rust is pretty.

My rust is prettier.

Penny Plastic Surgery

Create a simple chemical reaction to give an old penny a facelift.

What You Need
Penny (or any copper-containing object) • Paper towel • Table salt • White vinegar • *Medicine dropper*

What You Do
Place the penny on a paper towel. Sprinkle some table salt on the penny. Then drip a few drops of vinegar onto the salted penny. Tear off a piece of the paper towel and use it to rub the penny. It will look shiny and new.

Why It Works
The vinegar (an acetic acid and water *solution*) and salt (a sodium chloride *compound*) react. This makes the hydrogen in the vinegar combine with the chloride in the salt, making a new substance: *hydrochloric acid.* That's a very strong acid that can be dangerous in high *concentrations*— that is, if a lot of salt is dissolved in the vinegar. No need to worry, though, you made a low concentration of just enough acid to remove a layer of the penny's surface. It removed the dull layer that hid the shiny copper that pennies are made of. Wash or wipe the penny clean to stop the reaction.

71

Going Where No Egg Has Gone Before

Amaze and astound your friends with a feat of chemistry they'll have to see to believe.

What You Need

Adult helper • Peeled hardboiled egg • Glass bottle with a neck slightly smaller than the egg • Paper towel • Matches

What You Do

Put the egg on the mouth of the bottle. It should not go all the way in, but it should be close. (You might need to test different-sized eggs with different-sized bottles.) Set the egg nearby. Tear off ¼ of the paper towel, and roll it lengthwise. Have an adult light one end of the roll with a match and carefully drop the burning paper towel and match in the bottle. (You want them to continue burning in the bottle.) Immediately set the egg back on the mouth of the bottle. Wait a few seconds. The fire will go out and the egg will be sucked—almost in slow motion—into the mouth of the bottle, down the neck, and then all the way to the bottle's base.

Why It Works

Nature seeks *equilibrium*—balance—that's why your ears pop when you go up in the mountains or on an airplane. The popping opens your ears to the lower air pressure. (It's better than your head popping!) Burning the matches in the bottle changes the pressure because *oxygen* is used up during the burning. Since the egg is blocking the mouth, the (relatively) high pressure outside the bottle pushes it in.

Fire Extinguisher

You can smother a flame without even touching it.

What You Need
Adult helper • Votive candle (very short, squat candle) • Medium-sized bowl • Baking soda • Lighter • White vinegar

What You Do
Put the candle in the center of the bowl. Pour a handful of baking soda around the candle, in a circle. Then have the adult use the lighter to light the candle's wick. Carefully pour the vinegar down the inside of the side of the bowl until all the baking soda is wet. (Don't let it splash onto the flame!) A nearly invisible gas will extinguish the flame.

Why It Works
For anything to burn, there have to be oxygen *molecules* nearby that are ready to combine with other *elements*. The products of the chemical *reaction* we call fire usually include a gas and energy (the flame). When *baking soda* and *vinegar* combine, they react and create *carbon dioxide* by taking available oxygen out of the air. That means no more oxygen for the fire, so it dies.

Just in case, Ma'am.

Dad.

73

Air Freshener Bubbles

If you can smell it, chemistry is involved. Test this theory with a scented bubble concoction!

What You Need

Cooking extracts (vanilla, almond, and/or mint) • *Medicine dropper* • Small cups (3-ounce) • Water • Liquid dish detergent • *Bubble blower* • Rubbing alcohol (optional)

What You Do

Add 20 drops of one extract in a small cup. Add 10 drops of water and 1 drop of liquid dish detergent. Dip the bubble blower into the concoction, remove it, and blow through it to create bubbles. You'll smell the extract strongly when the bubbles burst. Use the same proportions to make a different batch of smelly bubbles.

Why It Works

Particular *molecules* in some plants have very strong aromas. You smell the aroma when these *volatile* molecules are released. This happens when a breeze blows past, or when something rubs against the plant. To make most cooking extracts, chemists extract (or remove) these molecules and place them in alcohol. The extract is *concentrated,* which means a little goes a long way.

If you want to make a cologne or perfume, mix drops of an extract with an equal amount of rubbing alcohol in a small cup. Dab the *concoction* on your wrists, neck, or ankles for a pleasant scent wherever you go. Be careful not to get it in your eyes.

Smell Ya Later!

Well, that about wraps it up. We hope you had fun with our chemistry concoctions. Don't forget to get your assistants to help you clean, and check to see if your lab coat is "dry-clean only" before throwing it in the wash. See you again…for sure!

Glossary

Acetic acid. An acid with a pungent odor that is the main component of vinegar.

Acetone. A flammable liquid with a distinct odor that is used as a solvent. (Some nail polish removers contain acetone.)

Acid. A compound, usually water-soluble, that reacts with a base to form a salt. Acids are corrosive and taste sour. Acids turn litmus paper red and anthocyanins red.

Acidic. Forming an acid in water and/or tasting sour.

Acid rain. Polluted rain containing dilute acid, resulting from burning fossil fuels (petroleum and coal).

Acid reaction. Chemical reaction in which an acid reacts with a base and creates a new substance.

Alcohol. An organic compound produced by the fermentation of sugar or starch and can be used as a solvent.

Alkali. A substance that is a base. It is water-soluble, neutralizes acids, and forms salts with acids. It turns litmus paper blue and anthocyanins blue.

Alkaline. Containing alkali or having is properties.

Anthocyanins. Water-soluble pigments that turn red when exposed to an acids substance and blue when exposed a base substance.

Atom. The basic particle of matter and the smallest portion an element can be divided into and remain an element.

Baking powder. A mixture of sodium bicarbonate, starch, and acids.

Baking soda. Sodium bicarbonate, a compound with a crystalline structure that is made from salts. It's a base and is used to neutralize acids.

Base. A chemical compound that reacts with acids to form salts. It tastes bitter and turns litmus paper and anthocyanins blue. See also alkali.

Basic. Relating to a base, or having a base (alkaline) reaction.

Bond. Chemical force holding atoms together in a compound.

Bubble blower. A simple device designed to be dipped in bubble-making concoctions and gently blown through, to create bubbles in desired shapes. Make a one by taking a pipe cleaner or wire and bending one end into a circle. If you have a circle at the end of a straight line, you made it correctly.

Calcium carbonate. A crystalline solid that's one of the world's most common natural substances.

Carbon. An element that exists in most organic compounds.

Carbonate. To make a liquid bubbly and gaseous by putting carbon dioxide into it.

Carbon dioxide. A heavy gas produced during animal respiration and also formed by chemical reactions.

Chemical reaction. See reaction.

Citric acid. An acid in fruit. It's used in canning and cleaning, and is sold in health food stores.

Colloid. A suspension of particles in another substance, or the particles suspended in another substance.

Compound. A substance made by chemically combining two or more elements.

Concentrate. A substance dissolved in another substance.

Concentration. The amount of a substance dissolved in another substance.

Concoction. A new or unusual substance created by mixing or combining ingredients.

Cross-link. A connection between parallel chains of a complex organic molecule, or to join polymer chains by a cross-link.

Crystalline. Clear and definite in shape, resembling crystals.

Crystal. A solid containing an internal pattern of atoms, molecules, or ions that is regular, repeated, and geometrically arranged.

Dense. Having relatively high mass per unit volume, indicating that molecules are closely packed.

Density. A measure of how much matter a unit of a substance contains, relative to the volume of the substance.

Desiccant. A substance that absorbs water and can be used to remove moisture.

Element. Any substance that cannot be broken down into a simpler one. There are more than 100 naturally occurring elements.

Epsom salts. Magnesium sulfate. It's used for medicinal purposes.

Equilibrium. A physical state of equality.

Evaporate. To change from a liquid to a gas over time.

Expand. To increase in size or volume.

Force. An influence that changes the arrangement of atoms, binding them or keeping them apart.

Funnel. Cone-shaped utensil with a small opening at the bottom and a larger opening at the top, used to guide substances into containers; the use of such a utensil. Make one by taking a half piece of paper and rolling up from one corner. Hold it together at the bottom as you use it.

Gas. A substance such as air that is neither a liquid nor a solid at ordinary temperatures and that has the ability to expand indefinitely.

Hydrochloric acid. A strong acid formed when hydrogen chloride gas breaks down in water.

Hydrogen. A gas that is the lightest chemical element and is the most abundant in the universe. It's in most organic compounds, and water.

Hydrogen bonding. An interaction between molecules of compounds when hydrogen atoms are bound to certain other atoms.

Indicator. A substance such as litmus or anthocyanin that shows the presence or concentration of an acid or base or of a particular material or chemical.

Inorganic. Chemical compounds that contain no carbon, with a few exceptions such as oxides of carbon.

Litmus paper. A piece of paper coated with a substance to indicate whether something is acid or base. It turns red in acids and blue in bases. Anthocyanin works the same way.

Liquid. A substance that is fluid at ordinary room temperature on Earth.

Glossary (continued)

Mass. How much a material weighs.

Matter. The material substance of the universe that has mass, weight, and occupies space.

Medicine dropper. A tool for dispensing small amounts of liquid. Can be substituted with a straw. Just dip one end of the straw into the liquid then put a finger over the other end. Hold it tight and a drop or more of the liquid will be caught in the straw. Release the finger on top to drop the liquid where you want it.

Mineral. Inorganic solid substance that occurs naturally in rock and in the ground.

Molecule. The smallest physical unit of a compound, consisting of one or more atoms held together by chemical bonds.

Monomers. Simple organic molecules that can join in long chains to form a complex molecule or polymer.

Neutral. Neither acidic nor alkaline.

Neutralize. To render another substance neither acid nor alkaline.

Nitrogen. An element that occurs as a gas. It's abundant in our atmosphere.

Organic compounds. Combinations of molecules that contain carbon. Most natural, living materials are organic compounds.

Oxidation. A reaction in which an element or compound combines with oxygen.

Oxidize. To react or cause a chemical to react with oxygen and form an oxide.

Oxygen. A gas that is an abundant element in the world and forms compounds with most elements.

Particles. A basic unit of matter, such as a molecule or atom.

Plasma. A hot gas found in the Sun, stars, and made by certain manmade chemical reactions.

Plastic. A manmade material made by creating polymers from organic compounds.

Polymer. A natural or manmade compound made of long chains of identical molecules called monomers.

Polystyrene. A manmade polymer that's made into a rigid foam.

Pressure. The force acting on a surface divided by the area over which it acts.

Reaction. A process that changes the molecular composition of a substance.

Salt. A crystalline compound formed by neutralizing an acid with a certain bases. Table salt, sodium chloride, is an edible salt with a tangy taste.

Saturation. A condition of a solution in which no more solute can be dissolved.

Seed crystal. A small crystal that will allow more of the same molecules to attach to its surface to grow a large crystal.

Sodium carbonate. A crystalline salt of carbonic acid used in soap and for many other uses.

Solid. A state of matter in which the substance exists in a fixed shape and resists moderate pressure.

Soluble. Able to be dissolved in a solvent.

Solute. A substance that dissolves in a solvent to create a solution.

Solution. A material made up of two or more substances mixed together uniformly, made by dissolving a solute in a solvent.

Solvent. A substance that dissolves a solute to create a solution.

Starch. An organic compound produced by plants.

State. The physical form of matter: liquid, solid, gas, or plasma.

Sulfate. A salt of sulfuric acid.

Sulfuric acid. A strong oily corrosive acid.

Supersaturation. The state of a chemical solution containing a greater amount of solute than normally possible, often as a result of heating then careful cooling.

Suspension. A dispersion of fine solid particles in a liquid.

Table salt. Sodium chloride, an edible salt with a tangy taste. See also salt.

Temperature. Measure of hot how a material is.

Vacuum. Emptiness caused by the removal of a gas.

Volatile. A substance that changes into a vapor at a relatively low temperature.

Volume. The space within or space occupied by a substance.

Water-Soluable. Capable of being dissolved completely by water.

Metric Conversions

To convert degrees Fahrenheit to degrees Celsius, subtract 32 and then multiply by .56.

To convert inches to centimeters, multiply by 2.5.

To convert ounces to grams, multiply by 28.

To convert teaspoons to milliliters, multiply by 5.

To convert tablespoons to milliliters, multiply by 15.

To convert fluid ounces to milliliters, multiply by 30.

To convert cups to liters, multiply by .24.

Acknowledgments

The molecules of our gratitude for **Jennifer Thomas** will expand indefinitely. Jennifer is a Nationally Board Certified Chemistry Teacher with both B.S. and Masters degrees. She consulted with us on how to craft creative concoctions, and patiently explained to us why each one works.

Tom LaBaff concocted a perfect look for this book with his hilarious illustrations. What a gas it's been to work with him.

We supersaturated Creative Director **Cella Naranjo** with the elements of this book. Celia, thank you for crystallizing the concept on each well-designed page—you created a gem.

Associate Editor **Rain Newcomb**, volatile as she is, could have vaporized each time we asked for help brainstorming the concoctions, their titles, and everything else. But she almost never did.

Basic Index

Baking science, 67

Carbon dioxide, 17, 20, 24, 25, 32, 42, 50, 55, 73

Crystals, 12, 13, 16, 17, 28, 29

Equilibrium, 72

Evaporation, 13, 15, 16

Density, 54, 55, 56

Fingerprint science, 33

Gas science, 43

Geyser science, 59

Lab rules, 10-11

Mummy science, 27

Polymers, 36, 38, 39, 40, 41, 44, 45, 57

Polymer science, 37

Pressure, 19, 42, 53, 62

Reactions, 17, 18, 20, 24, 25, 32, 35, 42, 46, 47, 50, 55, 58, 65, 73

Safety. *See* Lab rules

Salt science. *See* Mummy science

Slime. *See* Polymers

Soap science, 51

Soda pop science, 18

Solutions, 12, 13, 14, 15, 16, 21, 22, 23, 28, 29, 44, 45, 74

Concoctions Index

Blob, 40

Bones, bendable, 30

Bubble-making, 21, 22, 23, 50, 74

Chicken bones, using, 30

Color-change, 46, 47, 48, 49, 64, 65

Crystal, 28, 29

Deflating, 63

Destructive, 44, 45, 52

Dough, 66

Edible, 12, 13, 46

Eggs, using, 31, 32, 61, 68, 72

Fizzing, 58, 73. *See also* Foaming

Floating, 54, 55, 56, 68

Foaming, 17, 19, 50. *See also* Fizzing

Fossil, 16

Heat-producing, 24

Indicator, 64, 65

Inflating, 20

Invisible ink, 34-35

Oozing, 36, 38, 39. *See also* Splattering

Paint, 60, 61

Projectile, 42

Rock candy, 12, 13

Scented, 74

Shrinking, 26

Slime, 36, 38, 39

Splattering, 25, 58, 62. *See also* Oozing

Stalactite, 14-15

Stalagmite, 14-15